G000135437

Amazing Animals
Great White Sharks

Barbara Balfour

WEIGL PUBLISHERS INC.

Published by Weigl Publishers Inc.
350 5th Avenue, Suite 3304
New York, NY 10118-0069

Amazing Animals series copyright © 2007
WEIGL PUBLISHERS INC. www.weigl.com
All rights reserved. No part of this publication
may be reproduced, stored in a retrieval
system, or transmitted in any form or by any
means, electronic, mechanical, photocopying,
recording, or otherwise, without the prior
written permission of the publisher.

COVER: The great white shark is one of the
most feared sea animals because of its large
size and fierce teeth.

Editor
Heather C. Hudak
Design and Layout
Terry Paulhus

Library of Congress Cataloging-in-Publication
Data

Balfour, Barbara.
  Great white sharks / Barbara Balfour.
    p. cm. – (Amazing animals series)
  ISBN 1-59036-391-4 (hard cover : alk.
paper) – ISBN 1-59036-397-3 (soft cover :
alk. paper)
  1. White shark–Juvenile literature. I. Title.
II. Series.
  QL638.95.L3B35 2006
  597.3'3–dc22

2005027267

Printed in the United States of America
2 3 4 5 6 7 8 9 0 12 11 10 09 08

About This Book

This book tells you all about great white sharks. Find out where they live and what they eat. Discover how people are working hard to protect them. You can also read about them in myths and legends from around the world.

Words in **bold** are explained in the Words to Know section at the back of the book.

Useful Websites

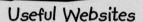

Addresses in this book take you to the home pages of websites that have information about great white sharks.

All of the Internet URLs given in the book were valid at the time of publication. However, due to the dynamic nature of the Internet, some addresses may have changed, or sites may have ceased to exist since publication. While the author and publisher regret any inconvenience this may cause readers, no responsibility for any such changes can be accepted by either the author or the publisher.

Contents

Meet the Great White Shark

Great white sharks are large, meat-eating fish. They are the most dangerous of all sharks.

The great white shark's skin is covered with a layer of tiny teeth called denticles. These denticles make the shark's skin feel like sandpaper.

▼ Great white sharks can swim fast because they have warmer body temperatures than other cold-blooded sharks.

Useful Websites

www.oceanofk.org/sharks/sharks.html

Learn more about sharks by visiting this website.

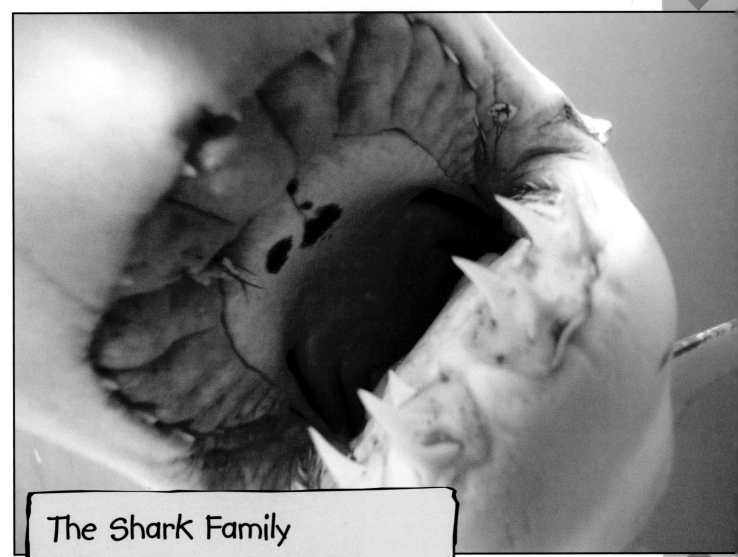

The Shark Family

There are 380 different kinds of sharks.

- angel sharks
- horn sharks
- megamouth sharks
- nurse sharks
- tiger sharks
- zebra sharks

▲ Great white sharks tear their food into mouth-sized pieces that they swallow whole.

A Very Special Animal

Great white sharks have five different kinds of fins. These fins help them swim and keep their balance.

A shark's bones can bend more easily than those of other fish. Shark bones are made out of soft **cartilage**, like the bendy part of human ears. This helps sharks to turn quickly when they swim.

Great white sharks have a sixth sense. They can sense **prey** from very far away using electrically sensitive **organs**. These organs are located on their head and help guide them toward prey.

▲ The great white shark's fierce appearance has earned it nicknames such as "man-eater" and "white death."

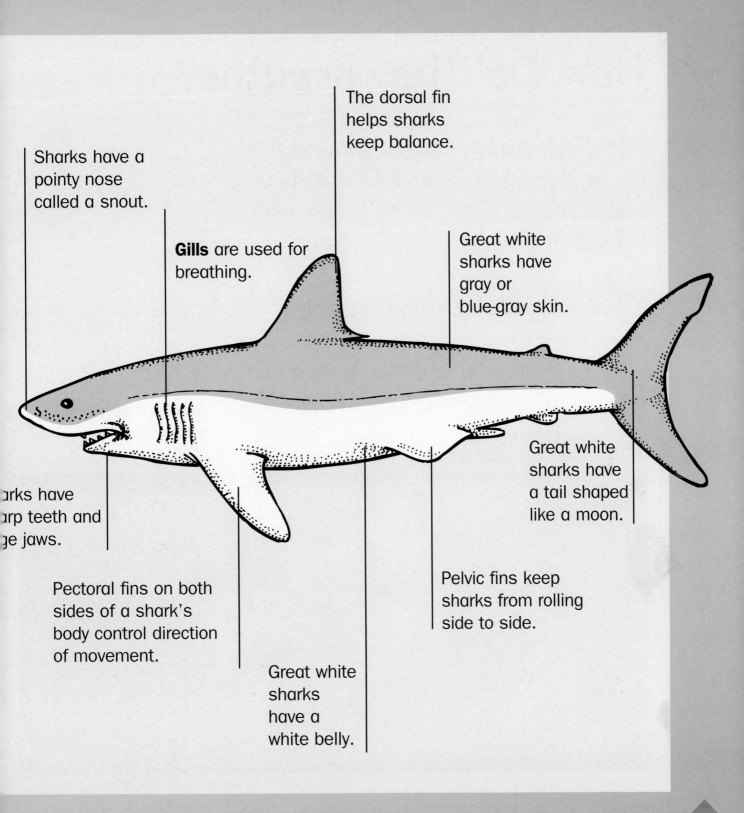

The dorsal fin helps sharks keep balance.

Sharks have a pointy nose called a snout.

Gills are used for breathing.

Great white sharks have gray or blue-gray skin.

Great white sharks have a tail shaped like a moon.

...arks have ...arp teeth and ...ge jaws.

Pectoral fins on both sides of a shark's body control direction of movement.

Pelvic fins keep sharks from rolling side to side.

Great white sharks have a white belly.

How Do They Breathe?

Great white sharks breathe through five, six, or seven gills on the side of their body. The openings can be found just behind their head.

Great white sharks swim with their mouth open so water can pass over the gills. The gills take in the oxygen in the water. Great white sharks then breathe out using their gills.

▼ A great white shark can smell one drop of blood in 25 gallons (100 liters) of water.

Breathing Facts

- Air holes on the side of the shark's head help keep sand out of the gills.

- A shark's snout is used to smell, but not to breathe.

- Great white sharks are the only sharks that can hold their heads above water.

▲ Most fish have their gills covered, but the great white shark's gills are open.

How Do They Eat?

All sharks are predators. They hunt other animals for food. Great white sharks are apex predators. This means they are at the top of the **food chain**. Great white sharks eat fatty animals, such as seals, octopuses, whales, and even other sharks.

Great white sharks do not fight each other for food. They may feed together or share their food.

▼ The great white shark attacks its prey, such as octopuses, from behind or below.

A Big Appetite

- Great white sharks do not chew. They bite and tear food using more than 3,000 teeth.

- Sharks have taste buds in their throats and all over their mouths.

- Sharks have an enormous liver. Their liver stores energy, in the form of oil. This helps them go without food for up to two months.

▲ A great white shark's teeth are lost and regrown thousands of times over a lifetime.

Where Do They Live?

Great white sharks live in coastal waters. They have been seen near the coasts of North America, Australia, and South Africa. Most great white sharks swim near the shore to find their prey.

In the fall, female great white sharks **migrate** to warmer waters. They do this to give birth to their pups. Warmer waters include the coasts of Florida and the Bahamas.

▼ A large meal can keep a great white shark well fed for up to 2 months.

Useful Websites

www.enchantedlearning.com

Search sharks on this website to learn more about where sharks live.

Great White Shark Range

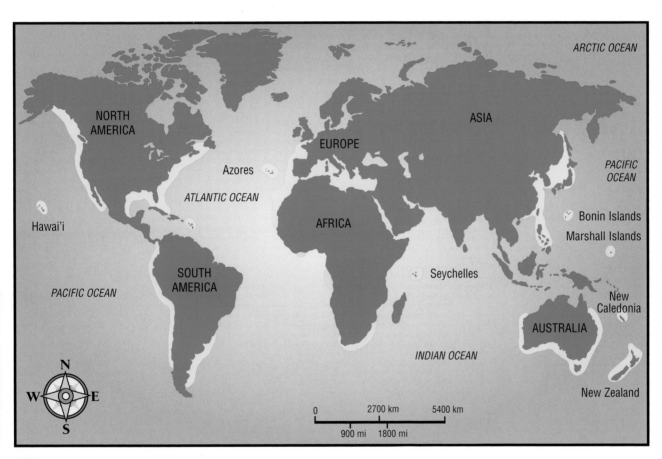

Known great white shark range

Friends and Enemies

Great white sharks and remora fish have a special relationship. Remoras eat **parasites** on the shark's skin. This prevents sharks from getting sick. The shark's presence scares away the remora's predators. This helps remoras survive. Killer whales are the only animals strong enough to attack sharks.

▼Remoras use sucker-like disks on their head to attach themselves to sharks.

Useful Websites

www.encyclopedia.com/
html/rl/remora.asp

Learn more about remoras by visiting this website.

Shark Talk

There are different ways sharks communicate with other animals.

• Sharks arch their back and drop their pectoral fins to warn off intruders. This action is called hunching.

• Gaping is when a shark lifts its head above water and opens its mouth. Scientists believe sharks do this to relieve stress or frustration.

▲ Great white sharks use two small sensors in their skull to hear their prey.

Growing Up

A female great white shark gives birth to live shark pups in the spring and summer. As many as 7 to 14 pups are part of one **litter**.

An unborn shark grows inside its mother's body for about one year. At birth, great white sharks can weigh up to 50 pounds (23 kilograms).

Pups learn to take care of themselves from birth. Great white sharks can live up to 30 years.

▶ When born, a shark pup is the same length and weight as a child in kindergarten.

Growth Chart

Some great white sharks grow to 21 feet (6 meters) long and weigh as much as 7,000 pounds (3,175 kg).

Most great white sharks are about the size of a family minivan, or 12 to 16 feet (4 to 5 m) long.

When a pup is born, it is about 4 feet (1.2 m) long and weighs about 40 pounds (18 kg).

▼ A young great white shark does not reach full maturity until it is 10 to 12 years old.

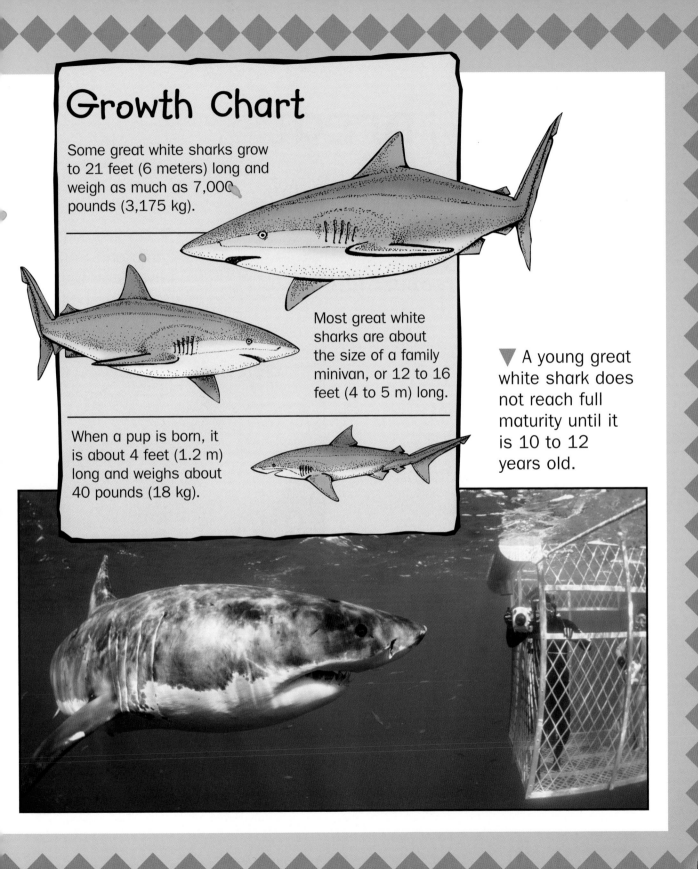

Under Threat

Humans hunt hundreds of sharks every year for fun, money, or food. Their teeth are used for necklaces. Their skin is made into leather. Shark fins are used to make soup.

▼ Bottles, tin cans, and traps have been found inside the bellies of great white sharks.

Great white sharks may become **extinct** if they are not protected. In 1991, South Africa became the first country to make hunting sharks illegal.

Useful Websites
www.kidzworld.com/site/
p4l88.htm

Find out how you can help sharks by visiting this website.

Sharks can still be harmed in other ways. Sometimes they get caught in fishing nets by accident and suffocate. Pollution from garbage and oil spills can harm sharks, too.

▲ Over the past 10 years, about 600,000 barrels of oil have accidentally spilled into seas and oceans each year.

What Do You Think?

Sharks have been known to attack humans. They also prey on animals that humans eat, such as seals and sea lions. If there were no more sharks, people and animals could use the ocean more safely. Should people be allowed to hunt sharks? Should people ensure sharks continue to live in the ocean with the other animals?

Myths and Legends

People have shared stories about sharks for hundreds of years. Popular movies, such as *Jaws*, show how people fear sharks.

Shark God

▲ Ancient Hawai'ians believed that the shark was the greatest *Aumakua*, or guardian angel.

People who lived in the Solomon and Fiji Islands believed the shark was a friendly god. They told stories of sharks who rescued lost fishermen and children who fell into the sea from their boats. They believed sharks were their friends and would not eat or hunt them.

From Sharks to Humans

Long ago, people who lived in Hawai'i believed that sharks could become humans. Today, there are people who worship sharks and believe sharks will protect them.

Giver of Light

People who lived in Fiji once believed that the son of their god was a shark named Dekuwaqa. He was also named Daucina, which means giver of light. It was believed that his body lit up at night to help guide the Fijians when they went to war.

▼ Great white sharks are often shown as deadly hunters. Shark attacks on humans are rare.

Quiz

1. What are shark bones made out of?
a) **cartilage** b) **muscle** c) **calcium**

2. What do sharks eat?
a) **plants** b) **water** c) **meat**

3. What is a baby shark called?
a) **a cub** b) **a pup** c) **a calf**

4. Which organ do sharks use to breathe?
a) **snout** b) **gills** c) **lungs**

5. Where do sharks live?
a) **river** b) **pond** c) **ocean**

Answers:

1. (a) Shark bones are made out of cartilage.
2. (c) Sharks eat meat.
3. (b) A baby shark is called a pup.
4. (b) Sharks use gills to breathe.
5. (c) Sharks live in the ocean.

Find out More

To find out more about the great white shark and how to keep it safe, visit the websites in this book. You can also write to the following organizations.

Shark Research Centre
South African Museum
P.O. Box 61
Cape Town 8000
South Africa

Shark Research Institute
P.O. Box 40
Princeton, NJ 08540

Ocean Conservancy
2029 K Street
Washington, DC 20006

Words to Know

cartilage
the bendy material that makes up a shark's skeleton

extinct
no longer living on Earth

food chain
plants and animals in a community linked together by what they eat

gills
organs that help fish to breathe underwater

litter
a group of newborn animals

migrate
to move from place to place depending on the season

organs
body parts

parasites
organisms that live on and feed off animals

prey
animals that are hunted by other animals for food

Index